TECHNOLOGIES
AND
STRATEGIES
IN BATTLE

THE BATTLE OF
YORKTOWN

Russell Roberts

Mitchell Lane
PUBLISHERS

P.O. Box 196
Hockessin, Delaware 19707
Visit us on the web: www.mitchelllane.com
Comments? email us: mitchelllane@mitchelllane.com

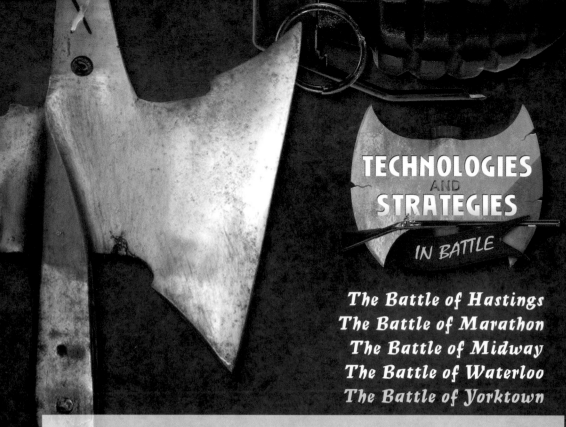

TECHNOLOGIES AND STRATEGIES
IN BATTLE

The Battle of Hastings
The Battle of Marathon
The Battle of Midway
The Battle of Waterloo
The Battle of Yorktown

PUBLISHER'S NOTE: The facts on which the story in this book is based have been thoroughly researched. Documentation of such research can be found on page 44. While every possible effort has been made to ensure accuracy, the publisher will not assume liability for damages caused by inaccuracies in the data, and makes no warranty on the accuracy of the information contained herein.

To reflect current usage, we have chosen to use the secular era designations BCE ("before the common era") and CE ("of the common era") instead of the traditional designations BC ("before Christ") and AD (*anno Domini*, "in the year of the Lord").

ABOUT THE AUTHOR: Russell Roberts has written and published nearly 40 books for adults and children, including *The Battle of Hastings* and *The Battle of Waterloo*. He lives in Bordentown, New Jersey, with his family and a fat, fuzzy, and crafty calico cat named Rusti.

Printing   1   2   3   4   5   6   7   8   9

Copyright © 2012 by Mitchell Lane Publishers

Library of Congress
Cataloging-in-Publication Data
Roberts, Russell, 1953-
 The Battle of Yorktown / by Russell Roberts.
     p. cm. — (Technologies and strategies in battle)
 Includes bibliographical references and index.
 ISBN 978-1-61228-074-5 (library bound)
 1. Yorktown (Va.)—History—Siege, 1781—
Juvenile literature. I. Title.
 E241.Y6.R59 2011
 973.3'37—dc22
                                                        2011000607
eBook ISBN: 9781612281568

PLB

CONTENTS

The sun had set on the town of York (eventually to be known as Yorktown), Virginia, and darkness was rapidly falling on this Sunday night. The allied American and French soldiers sat in trenches outside York and waited for the signal to attack the British troops just 150 yards (45 meters) away from them.

Many of the waiting troops spent the time making sure that their bayonets were attached firmly and correctly to their muskets. Their commander, General George Washington, wanted to make sure that the attack was a complete surprise. He had ordered total silence among his troops; no soldier could even load his musket until he had reached his destination. The attackers would use their bayonets instead.

Now, as the troops waited, some possibly marveled at the approximately one-foot- (30-centimeter-) long blade of tempered steel with which they were about to charge across the ground. The bayonet charge was an important part of the British Army's strategy during the American Revolution. British soldiers would fire one volley and then charge at the colonials with their bayonets aimed and ready.[1] It took an exceptionally

Bayonet Night Attack!

brave man to stand his ground against all that steel coming at him like a thousand tiger fangs. Now, however, it was the allies' turn to give the British a taste of their own medicine.

Although the night was moonless, high in the western sky the planets Jupiter and Venus gleamed brightly. They were so close together this night that when a Continental soldier named Joseph Plumb Martin looked at them, he thought it was a flare signaling the attack. Heart beating furiously, he was about to leap to his feet when he realized it was not the signal—just two bright planets. He settled down, trying to calm his pounding heart.

The British commander, Lieutenant General Lord Charles Cornwallis, had brought his army of 7,500 British troops to Yorktown in early August. With

its deep harbor, Yorktown was perfect for a British relief force to sail to the rescue of his weary and hungry soldiers. But days had turned into weeks, and no British ships had arrived.

Washington, commander of the 17,000-man allied army, had marched down from the New York City area to attack Cornwallis at Yorktown. However, once he arrived, Washington had decided upon a new strategy instead of an all-out attack: a siege.

Ever since October 9, Washington had been besieging the British forces in Yorktown, and he knew it was taking its toll.

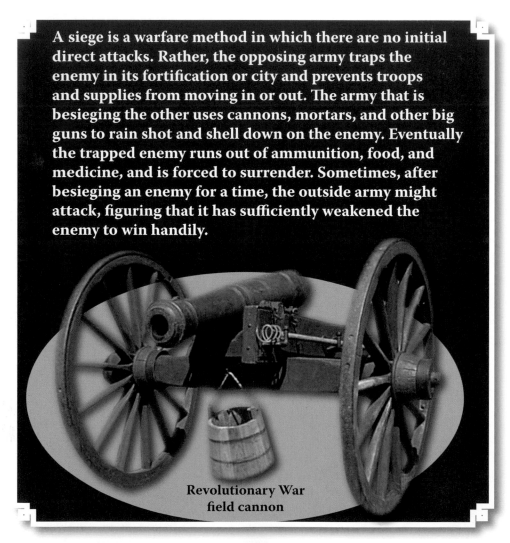

A siege is a warfare method in which there are no initial direct attacks. Rather, the opposing army traps the enemy in its fortification or city and prevents troops and supplies from moving in or out. The army that is besieging the other uses cannons, mortars, and other big guns to rain shot and shell down on the enemy. Eventually the trapped enemy runs out of ammunition, food, and medicine, and is forced to surrender. Sometimes, after besieging an enemy for a time, the outside army might attack, figuring that it has sufficiently weakened the enemy to win handily.

Revolutionary War
field cannon

The York River was clogged with the bodies of hundreds of horses floating downstream. The British had killed them so that they would not have to use precious food on the animals.[2]

The allied armies kept creeping closer and closer to the British, digging trenches in which their soldiers could take cover and moving their artillery into better firing positions. It was dangerous work, because the British would shoot the men who were digging the trenches and setting up the guns. As Continental soldiers were working on the night of October 3, a single British cannonball killed four of them.

In order to extend the trenches even closer, two British redoubts—9 and 10—had to be taken. Redoubt 9 held 120 English soldiers, while number 10 had 70. Around 2 P.M. on Sunday, October 14, 1781, Washington ordered an attack on both posts just after dark. Backed by cannon fire, four hundred French soldiers would attack Redoubt 9, and the same number of Americans would storm number 10.

Earlier that day, Washington had visited both sets of attacking troops. Normally he did not give battlefield speeches, but this time he spoke to the Americans, telling them to be brave. The men listened nervously. Captain Stephen Olney of Rhode Island

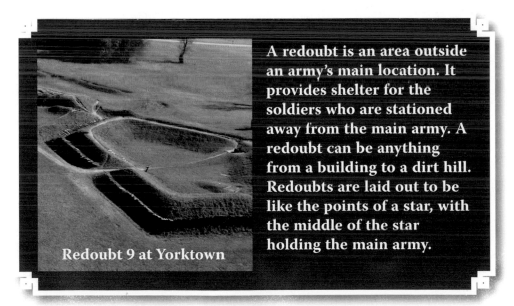

Redoubt 9 at Yorktown

A redoubt is an area outside an army's main location. It provides shelter for the soldiers who are stationed away from the main army. A redoubt can be anything from a building to a dirt hill. Redoubts are laid out to be like the points of a star, with the middle of the star holding the main army.

said: "I thought then that His Excellency's knees rather shook, but I have since doubted whether it was not mine."[3]

At 6:30 P.M., as planned, some French troops began firing to divert British attention. Thirty minutes later the attack signal came. The soldiers scrambled out of their trenches and advanced in the gloom. All knew that at any moment, a bullet could come hurtling through the darkness and cut them down.

The French troops had gone about 125 steps when a voice called out to them in German. It was a Hessian soldier—a German fighting for the British. Without replying, the French continued moving forward. All at once the darkness ahead of them exploded with sound and light; the British had opened fire! The air was thick with musket balls. Men started dropping as they were struck.

Meanwhile, the American attackers had gotten almost all the way to Redoubt 10 without being detected. Suddenly they stopped, surprised. The earlier artillery fire had barely damaged the redoubt. Groups of razor-sharp wooden stakes called abatises bristled before them like deadly porcupine quills; a man could easily get caught on or even killed by them. If nothing else, they

A re-creation of Redoubt 9 shows how the abatis protected the soldiers from a charge. Abatises, which date from Roman times, are rarely used in battle anymore, mainly because they can be destroyed by fire. Wire fortifications are usually used in their place.

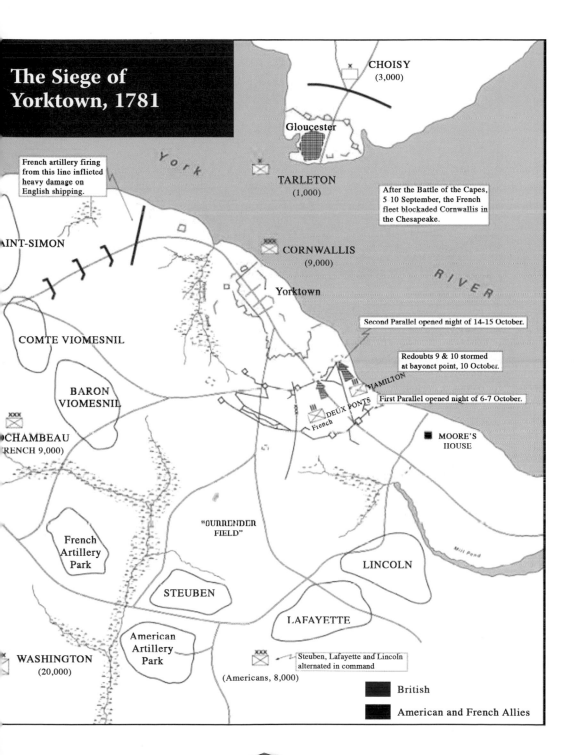

The Siege of Yorktown, 1781

CHOISY
(3,000)

Gloucester

York

French artillery firing from this line inflicted heavy damage on English shipping.

TARLETON
(1,000)

After the Battle of the Capes, 5 10 September, the French fleet blockaded Cornwallis in the Chesapeake.

AINT-SIMON

CORNWALLIS
(9,000)

Yorktown

RIVER

Second Parallel opened night of 14-15 October.

COMTE VIOMESNIL

Redoubts 9 & 10 stormed at bayonet point, 10 October.

BARON VIOMESNIL

HAMILTON

First Parallel opened night of 6-7 October.

DEUX PONTS
French

MOORE'S HOUSE

CHAMBEAU
(RENCH 9,000)

"SURRENDER FIELD"

French Artillery Park

LINCOLN

Mill Pond

STEUBEN

LAFAYETTE

American Artillery Park

Steuben, Lafayette and Lincoln alternated in command

WASHINGTON
(20,000)

(Americans, 8,000)

British

American and French Allies

The American assault on Redoubt 10 was a key moment in the Battle of Yorktown. If the assault had failed, the British would have maintained this key position, putting Washington's entire siege strategy in jeopardy.

forced the attackers to halt. Moments later the redoubt erupted in a sheet of flame as the British opened fire on the advancing Americans.

Washington watched the struggle with great concern. He saw the Americans fall as the British volley tore into them. He knew that everything depended on the success of this attack. If the British held the redoubts, then they could stop the allies from advancing their trenches any farther. The whole siege could fail.

Generals Washington and Rochambeau look out from the trenches at Yorktown toward the British positions. A collapsible telescope helped them see things at a distance.

"Sir," said Colonel David Cobb, an aide to Washington, "you are too much exposed here. Had you not better step a little back?"

"Colonel Cobb," Washington replied, "if you are afraid, you have liberty to step back."[4]

Washington turned his attention back to the battle. The screams of dying and wounded men rang in his ears, along with the popping sound of gunfire.

Would the allies be successful? Or would the British beat them back?

The Bayonet

No one knows exactly how the bayonet originated. According to legend, in seventeenth-century Spain, a group of Basques fighting for independence found themselves out of ammunition and surrounded by Spanish soldiers. Desperately one of the Basques jammed his knife—known as a *bayonnette*—into the muzzle of his musket. Others did the same thing, and suddenly the Basques had spear-type weapons that they could use to fight off the Spanish soldiers at close quarters. The place where this supposedly occurred is now Bayonne, France.

It is more likely that the bayonet originated because of the need to protect soldiers who fired muskets. When the musket was invented, it took a long time to reload it. This made soldiers defenseless against attacks by enemy troops, who merely had to wait until a musket was fired to attack. To defend the soldier who fired the musket, soldiers with spears or pikes were placed next to them.

However, this caused quite a manpower drain on an army, because essentially two soldiers were being used to do the job of one. Thus the bayonet was developed: after a soldier fired his musket, he jammed the bayonet into the muzzle of his musket. Now he had a weapon he could use to defend himself. This type of bayonet evolved throughout the seventeenth century.

Since these bayonets

A French muzzle bayonet

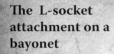
The L-socket attachment on a bayonet

went into the muzzle, they made it impossible to fire the gun. Thus a new generation of bayonets was developed that locked into place—usually by means of an L-shaped notch—in a sleeve or socket attached to the barrel. This left the gun's muzzle clear for reloading and firing.

By the time of the American Revolution, most bayonets were similar to the British model. This was known as the Long Land bayonet, named after the Long Land musket (nicknamed the Brown Bess). The blade was 16 to 17 inches (41 to 43 centimeters) long and square at the base.

When the French entered the war, the bayonet was altered to match those used by French soldiers. This bayonet was shorter—about 14 inches (36 centimeters) long—and curved at the base.

A re-creation of a bayonet with an L-socket.

By the start of 1781, the American Revolution that had begun with such hope six years before seemed to be on the verge of flickering out.

The soul-stirring days of 1775–76, and American victories at places such as Lexington and Concord and Trenton, were distant memories. George Washington's army now consisted of just a few thousand men, many clothed in rags and barefoot, who lived on scraps of food.

The individual states, which were supposed to provide men and supplies for the national army, had sent barely anything. The Continental Congress was bankrupt and of no help. In January 1781, Washington had written in his diary: "In a word, instead of having everything in readiness to take the field, we have nothing."[1]

Like much else in the Continental army, guns and ammunition were in short supply. While some soldiers and officers carried pistols, the musket was the typical firearm of that era. Since muskets were single-shot weapons, they had to be reloaded every time they were fired. There were numerous steps involved in loading and firing a musket, and a soldier

Muskets and Long Rifles

who could fire three shots in a minute was considered good. Soldiers had to learn and practice how to fire one so that they could do it as quickly as possible. While the British troops had enough muskets and ammunition for daily training, few colonial soldiers had that opportunity.

The musket was loaded with cartridges, made by soldiers in camp. Cartridges were a combination of lead, paper, and black powder—and if they got wet they were useless. The soldier carried them in a cartridge box, whose critical function was to keep the cartridges dry. Soldiers without cartridge boxes or with boxes that were ripped, torn, or otherwise damaged were at a serious disadvantage during battle.

All of these things—muskets, cartridges, and cartridge

The primary functions of a cartridge box were to carry cartridges and keep them dry. A wet cartridge was worthless to a soldier.

boxes—were in short supply for George Washington's army. The British, on the other hand, were usually well supplied with these items. A discouraged George Washington wrote desperately in early 1781 to the governors of the New England states, begging for food, clothing, money—anything. Unless they responded, Washington noted darkly, "the worst that can befall us may be expected."[2]

England was hoping for exactly that result, and was doing everything possible to achieve it with a new war strategy. The British generals felt that by focusing on the poorly defended southern colonies, an area they felt was heavy with British sympathizers (known as Tories or Loyalists), they could easily win the war. Once the southern colonies were back under British rule, the rebellion would wither and die in those few northern states still fighting, like a leaf withers after being cut off from a branch. Instead of engaging Washington and his troops in the northern colonies, the British were concentrating on the south and letting Washington sit with his army outside British-occupied New York City.

It didn't seem likely that England would have to fire any more shots at Washington. Their southern strategy was proving highly successful. By the end of 1780, they had already taken Savannah (Georgia), Charleston (South Carolina), and Camden (South Carolina).

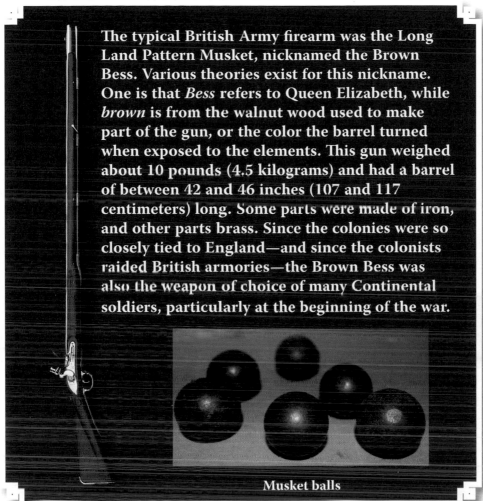

The typical British Army firearm was the Long Land Pattern Musket, nicknamed the Brown Bess. Various theories exist for this nickname. One is that *Bess* refers to Queen Elizabeth, while *brown* is from the walnut wood used to make part of the gun, or the color the barrel turned when exposed to the elements. This gun weighed about 10 pounds (4.5 kilograms) and had a barrel of between 42 and 46 inches (107 and 117 centimeters) long. Some parts were made of iron, and other parts brass. Since the colonies were so closely tied to England—and since the colonists raided British armories—the Brown Bess was also the weapon of choice of many Continental soldiers, particularly at the beginning of the war.

Musket balls

The British commander in the south, forty-three-year-old Lord Cornwallis, was an aggressive general. He was short and heavyset, with graying hair and a bad eye as a result of a sports injury suffered in his youth. Throughout 1780, he had rolled up victories in the south. To try to stop him, Washington picked General Nathanael Greene to command all American forces from Delaware to Georgia.

When Greene took over the southern Continental army, it consisted of 2,307 infantrymen—on paper. In reality, there were just 1,482 men present for duty, with only 800 of those properly

clothed and equipped.³ Among those soldiers was one of the Americans' most dangerous weapons: the frontiersman with his legendary Kentucky rifle, also known as the Pennsylvania rifle or the long rifle.

American and British forces in the south clashed at the Battle of Kings Mountain and then at Cowpens, both of which were American victories. Greene then fought Cornwallis at the Battle

A musket was a smoothbore gun—that is, there were no grooves in its barrel. When the musket ball was fired, it tended to bounce around inside the barrel on its way out. This made the musket accurate to a distance of only 50 to 100 yards (15 to 30 meters). When using a musket, it was critical to fire fast and in massed volleys.

Rifling—putting grooves inside the barrel—greatly increased the accuracy of firearms. The long rifle was probably developed sometime in the 1740s on the American frontier, born from the need to accurately shoot game for food or an enemy for survival. Because the smoothbore musket was terribly inaccurate, a reliable firearm was a welcome invention.

Around 1725, German craftsmen in Pennsylvania designed an early form of the long rifle.⁴ These rifles had grooves cut into the inside of the barrel. When the gun was fired, the grooves spun a lead ball as it was shot out of the barrel. This spinning action made the shot extremely accurate.

of Guilford Courthouse in North Carolina on March 15, 1781. Although the battle was a victory for Cornwallis, it might as well have been a defeat, for his army was seriously crippled; more than a quarter of the 1,900 British troops were either killed or wounded, including numerous officers. American casualties were much lighter—78 killed and 183 wounded. As British politician

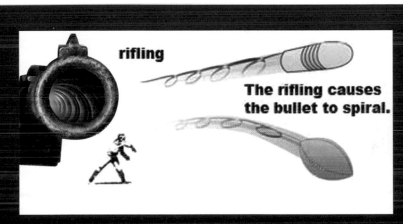

rifling

The rifling causes the bullet to spiral.

American frontiersmen took this gun and extended the barrel to be anywhere from 3 to 4 feet (about a meter) long, making the gun usually about 6 feet (nearly 2 meters) long. The wood stock was made out of maple, cherry, or walnut.

In the hands of a skilled marksman, the long rifle could be accurate to a range of 250 to 300 yards (76 to 91 meters). The British had a healthy respect for the accuracy of the rifleman, because they knew that the gun's deadly accuracy and great range made them a target from almost anywhere on the battlefield. Certainly the rifle had its disadvantages—it was slow to load, and it had no bayonet attachment, so riflemen needed a defensive weapon such as a tomahawk during an enemy charge—but more often than not the rifle dealt out death.

Tomahawk

Charles Fox said sarcastically: "Another such victory would ruin the British Army."[5]

That night, after the battle, Cornwallis pitched his tent on the rainy battlefield. All around him in the darkness he could hear the moans of his dying and wounded men.[6] He thought long and hard about his campaign to subdue the southern colonies. It was impossible to find food to feed his army there. He had not been able to destroy Greene's army, and the flame of independence still burned in the south.

The next day, as more men perished from their wounds, Cornwallis found that he had only about 700 men in fighting condition and nearly double that number in the hospital.[7] It was possibly around this time that he first thought of going to Virginia. It made sense to him: Virginia was the largest and most powerful state, and it supplied food and weapons for the Americans. The south—maybe even America itself—would never be conquered if the British could not conquer Virginia.

Cornwallis began a 200-mile (320-kilometer) march—some call it a retreat—to Wilmington, North Carolina, on the coast. Greene and his army immediately took advantage of Cornwallis's absence and began reclaiming areas in the Carolinas that he had abandoned.

During his march to Wilmington, the idea of conquering Virginia seemed better and better to Cornwallis. Without obtaining approval from General Henry Clinton, his superior officer in New York City, Cornwallis entered Virginia early in May 1781. Little did he know he had taken a huge step in helping America gain independence.

General Cornwallis

Loading A Musket

In the heat of battle, with enemy soldiers firing and charging, a soldier had to be able to load his musket as automatically as he drew a breath or he would not be breathing long. Speed of firing was the key for muskets; accuracy was secondary.

The steps for loading and firing a musket were as follows:

1. Prime and Load—The soldier took a quarter right turn and brought the musket to the priming position.
2. Handle Cartridge—The soldier pulled a cartridge from his cartridge box, bit the paper top off, and covered it with his thumb.
3. Prime—The soldier shook a bit of the black powder from the cartridge into the pan at the back of the barrel so that it was ready to ignite, then closed a metal piece called a frizzen to trap the powder.
4. About—The soldier dropped the butt end of the musket to the ground, then put the rest of the powder from the cartridge into the muzzle. He dropped in the metal ball, then used the paper to plug the muzzle so that the ball would not roll out.

Musket cartridge

5. Draw Ramrods—The soldier pulled the wood or steel ramrod from the bottom of the musket.
6. Ram Down the Cartridge—The soldier pushed the ramrod down into the barrel of the musket, forcing the ball, paper, and black powder down as far as they could go.
7. Return Ramrod—The soldier slid the ramrod back under the gun.
8. Present—The soldier brought the musket up, balanced it against his shoulder, pulled back the hammer, and was ready to fire.

Try doing that fast when you're under attack!

For a long time George Washington's strategy was to have the Americans and their French allies attack British-held New York City. The French were not interested in this idea.

At first the alliance with France had seemed like the answer to America's prayers. By themselves the thirteen former colonies might not have been able to defeat powerful England. With the assistance of England's traditional enemy France, however, America's odds greatly improved.

The new partnership between America and France had gotten off to a shaky start. Four thousand French troops had landed in Newport, Rhode Island, in July 1780. However, Washington did not meet with the French commander, Jean-Baptiste-Donatien de Vimeur, Comte de Rochambeau, until September. For months the French soldiers sat idle and unhappy in a strange city in a strange country. "We are vegetating at the very door of the enemy . . . ," a French officer had complained, "we are of no possible aid to our allies."[1]

In May 1781, the two commanders held a conference at Wethersfield, Connecticut, to

Two Strategies

plan a joint offensive. They considered two possible strategies: either attack British-occupied New York City, or go south to Virginia and fight Cornwallis. Meanwhile, in April, Washington had sent the Marquis de Lafayette to Virginia with a tiny army of about 1,000 men. Badly outnumbered by Cornwallis, Lafayette could only avoid him as the two armies ranged over Virginia.

Rochambeau argued for a Virginia campaign, but it wouldn't be easy. Washington knew that American troops from the north were suspicious of the southern climate, feeling that it would have a bad effect on their health. It would be difficult to get them to march south—many would desert, he thought, over fear of the Virginia weather—while New York City was much closer. Washington thought that

the best strategy would be for the allies to attack New York City. The British commander there, Sir Henry Clinton, would almost certainly recall troops from Cornwallis to help fend off the attack. Thus Lafayette would be helped and New York City would possibly be liberated.

Rochambeau knew that Clinton had over 14,000 soldiers well barricaded in New York, and that an attack on the British there would be hard and bloody. Cornwallis, on the other hand, had just over 7,000 in Yorktown, and many of those were wounded and could not fight.

There was a wild card in all this planning, and that was that a large French fleet of twenty-eight ships under command of Admiral François-Joseph-Paul, Comte de Grasse, was on its way from the West Indies. It would arrive off the U.S. coast in either July or August, be joined by ten other French vessels, and be available for joint military operations against the British. Finally, here was a fleet powerful enough to stand up against the mighty British Navy.

Although Washington had command of the combined French and American land forces, he had no control over the French fleet, and he could only urge it to sail to the New York area. Rochambeau, however, was able to communicate with de Grasse directly. Even though he agreed with Washington that New York City should be the target, he wrote to de Grasse: "it will be there [Virginia] where we think you may be able to render the greatest service."[2] This type of wording practically guaranteed that de Grasse would head to Virginia and not New York City.

Although he might have differed with Washington over strategy, Rochambeau was extremely sympathetic to the American cause. In another letter to de Grasse, Rochambeau urged the admiral to bring soldiers and money with him, since he knew that Washington desperately needed both: "I must not conceal from you, Monsieur, that the Americans are at the end of their resources."[3] He also wrote: "This is the state of affairs and the great crisis at which America finds itself."[4]

The Battle of Long Island, also known as the Battle of Brooklyn, was fought in August 1776. When Washington pulled out his troops after the battle, the British moved in and occupied New York City. They stayed there until the end of the war.

In early August, 1781, the French marched down from Newport, Rhode Island, to join Washington's army at White Plains, New York. Washington had promised to have 10,000 men plus militia ready to fight. Instead he had just several thousand. "They told us at Newport that the American army had 10,000 men," said a French soldier. "It has 2500 or 3000 men, and that is not much of a lie for the Americans."[5]

For the next week or so, Washington and Rochambeau, accompanied by their staffs, made a thorough inspection of the British defenses surrounding New York City. The two generals

There were many different styles of uniforms and forms of dress in the American Revolution, and it was sometimes difficult to determine friend from foe by their clothing. The British redcoats were the exception. Their bright uniforms made them easy targets for militia marksmen.

sometimes spent twenty-four straight hours riding around in the summer heat.

On August 14, 1781, Washington received word that de Grasse could remain in Chesapeake Bay only until October 15, when he had orders to return to the West Indies. Washington had to decide which strategy he would pursue. Would he stay with his dream of recapturing New York City? Or would he gamble that the French fleet would arrive off Virginia without incident, that the British Navy would not disrupt it, that Lord Cornwallis would remain where he was at Yorktown, and that the combined American-French army could make it down to Yorktown before the British in New York City figured out what was going on? If they caught on to Washington's strategy, they might either send reinforcements to Cornwallis or attack the allied army as it tried to head south.

Washington made his decision. On August 21, the combined armies began marching to Virginia.

Uniforms of the Revolution

One of the big differences between the French and Continental armies was their uniforms. The French had complete uniforms that included a white shirt, black neck stock (worn around the neck over the shirt collar), white-sleeved waistcoat, white breeches (a type of pants), and either white or black gaiters (worn over the leg from about the knee down to the ankle). Their shoes were black. Overall, the French were color coordinated and extremely well dressed.

On the other hand, the Americans wore a hodgepodge of clothing; many did not have much to wear at all. (A few months before, General Greene had complained that his soldiers were "almost naked . . . and barefoot."[6]) Although Washington had ordered that uniforms were to be dark blue, with markings identifying each state, the army's perpetual shortage of clothing made that impossible. Clothing varied from soldier to soldier, from smart-looking to raggedy. As one uniform expert wrote, "The army was . . . clothed . . . only as supplies permitted . . . [and] it varied sharply from comparative smartness to near-nakedness."[7]

Many men wore a hunting shirt, modeled after Native American clothing. They were made of unbleached homespun, deerskin, or linen, which could be dyed different colors depending upon the soldier's regiment. Sometimes this "Indian" dress included fringed deerskin leggings and moccasins. Washington heartily approved of this style of dress, saying, "If I were left to my own inclination, I should not only order the men to adopt the Indian dress, but cause the officers to do it also, and be the first to set the example myself."[8]

The allied armies that began the long march to Virginia were very different from each other in appearance. The French looked, as writer Robert Leckie remarked, like a "moving flower garden,"[1] with their colorful uniforms, flags, and feathers in their hats. The Americans, on the other hand, had no uniforms; many were barefoot, and much of their clothing was torn, tattered, and dirty.

Few except Washington and Rochambeau knew the enormous task these men were undertaking. Most of the soldiers considered it just another march, like the one before and the one to come next. American officer Alexander Hamilton thought the march was a wild goose chase.[2]

One clue to the march's importance was that Washington had forbidden women to come along. It was common at this time for women to live with soldiers (some as husband and wife, some not), cook and sew for the army, and march right along with them. The ban on women indicated that this march was deadly serious.[3]

Washington knew full well the significant implications of his move south. If the French fleet did not show up outside

The March South

Yorktown as promised . . . if the French fleet were defeated by the English . . . if Clinton in New York sent thousands of reinforcements to Cornwallis . . . if Cornwallis left Yorktown . . . if Clinton guessed what the allies were up to, came out of New York, and attacked them en route—any one of these scenarios might well spell defeat and possibly the end of the American Revolution.

Washington did all he could to ensure success. Knowing that the information would get back to the British because of Tories and spies, he built a fake camp near Chatham, New Jersey. It was the perfect launching pad for an attack on New York. He had large ovens built as evidence for feeding a big army. He talked about Staten Island with a farmer who was a known Tory. He sent out fake messages with

details about a planned attack, knowing that they would likely fall into enemy hands.

In their efforts to keep Clinton bottled up in New York City, the allies were helped by Clinton himself. The British commander was perpetually nervous, always feeling that he didn't have enough troops in case of attack, even though his army sat behind strong defenses. He was comfortable in the city and didn't want to do anything to disturb his position. He found any excuse not to send troops to Cornwallis at Yorktown.

Clinton's orders to Cornwallis were a blizzard of contradictions and possibilities. William Franklin (son of Benjamin), who had sided with the British, called Clinton's plans "unintelligible."[4] This confusion frustrated and annoyed Cornwallis, who was trying to sell Clinton on his plan of attacking Virginia. The two generals sniped at each other in their letters; their animosity kept them from working together to attack the allies.

But while Clinton dillydallied, others suspected that Washington was up to something. Clinton began receiving reports from spies and Tories that the allies were heading south. Still, he hesitated. On August 27, he wrote Cornwallis that he could not figure out what Washington was doing. He thought that the American was returning to his former camp in Morristown, New Jersey.[5]

Finally, on September 2, 1781, like a sleeper waking up, Clinton suddenly realized Washington's goal. He sent an urgent letter to Cornwallis, warning him of Washington's southward troop movement. But it was too late.

At Yorktown, Cornwallis was under no illusions about his position, calling it "not . . . very strong."[6] Yet he always felt that the superior British Navy would be able to rescue him at some point.

However, the British admirals in America were just as lax as Clinton. The first was Vice Admiral Marriot Arbuthnot, whom one writer described as "an aging, vacillating, irritable has-been."[7] He was replaced by Sir Thomas Graves, who was only slightly better. In mid-August, 1781, urged to sail his fleet out of New

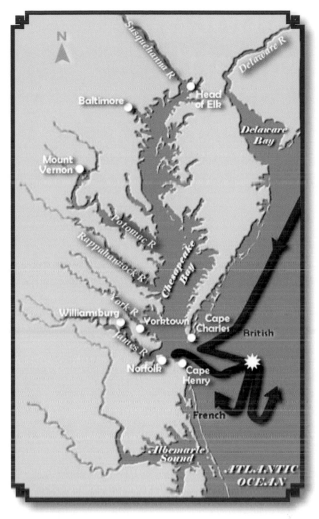

The British Navy sailed down from New York City to Chesapeake Bay, meeting the French on September 5.

York harbor and out to sea to find the French fleet, Graves responded with a laundry list of problems that prevented him from sailing: this ship was leaky, that one needed its masts replaced, and so on.

On September 1, Admiral Graves finally got his ships in motion and headed southward. On the morning of September 5, he found the French fleet under de Grasse in Chesapeake Bay. The climactic battle of the war—the one that would determine the fate of America—was about to begin.

A Critical Sea Battle

On September 5, 1781, an open-water battle was fought outside Chesapeake Bay. The British fleet of 19 ships, with Admiral Thomas Graves commanding, encountered the French fleet of 24 warships under Admiral de Grasse. Although they had superior numbers, the French were not the best sailors—their ships sometimes collided, but the French high command felt that an occasional collision was okay. The English, on the other hand, were masters of the sea.

When the French were sighted, their ships were inside the bay. The English could have easily bottled them up in the bay and either attacked their ships one by one as they tried to escape or done nothing, leaving them floating harmlessly in the Chesapeake.

However, Graves was operating under what were known as the Fighting Instructions. These were strict British rules for fighting naval battles, and commanders who disobeyed them were court-martialed, imprisoned, and even executed. These rules called for an attack in a certain manner, and to do that the French needed to be out in the open water facing the English. Graves allowed de Grasse to slowly bring his ships out of the bay and into the Atlantic and get into fighting formation. At any moment Graves could have attacked, but he did not.

Navy bar shots were fired from cannons. They were designed to rip sails and rigging and immobilize the opposition.

Cannons on board a ship had to fire through an opening in the side of the ship. This limited the cannons' maneuverability and made them inviting targets for the gunners on the opposing ship.

When the battle finally occurred, it was late afternoon. With only a few hours left to fight, the two sides volleyed using hundreds of guns, with the French inflicting more damage than the English. Over the next few days, with their ships too damaged to engage, both fleets drifted south until they lost sight of each other. The French sailed back to Chesapeake Bay, and the English sailed to New York for repairs. The victorious French now controlled the seas, and Cornwallis was stuck without supplies or reinforcements at Yorktown. Realizing the battle's significance, England's King George III cried out in despair, "I nearly think the empire ruined . . ."[8]

Cartridge

Angels

Shot in the form of pineapples

Bomb

inside

Cartouches or canister shot

Chain shot

Once Clinton finally realized the danger Cornwallis was in, he put 4,000 soldiers and 20 days' food for 8,000 men aboard ships, ready to sail for Yorktown.[1] However, whether or not they could get to Cornwallis depended upon which nation controlled the ocean—England or France. Graves' defeat on September 5 ended any hope of getting the supplies to Cornwallis.

Meanwhile, Cornwallis hunkered down in Yorktown. It seems unbelievable that he would do nothing to disrupt the allies as they slowly closed the trap around him. However, he always felt that, at any moment, British ships would sail into the harbor and rescue him. As he wrote to Clinton on September 16:

> If I had no hopes of relief, I would rather risk an action than defend my half finished works [fortifications] . . . but . . . I do not think myself justified in putting the fate of the war on so desperate an attempt.[2]

However, Cornwallis also knew that he could not hold out long. In the same letter he wrote: "This place [Yorktown] is in no

Siege at Yorktown

state of defense. If you cannot relieve me very soon, you must be prepared to hear the worst."[3]

When Clinton received this letter, he interpreted "the worst" to mean nothing more than a retreat . . . not surrender.[4] The idea of relieving Cornwallis was critically important, but no one seemed to be in much of a hurry. Admiral Graves, who had returned to New York after losing to de Grasse, initially said the navy would be ready to try another relief attempt by October 5. Then, on September 30, he informed Clinton that, because of repairs, his ships would not be ready until October 12. It would then be at least another week or more—if they succeeded in defeating the French—before they could get to Cornwallis.

On September 28, the allied army arrived at Yorktown. Washington knew the area

well—as a youngster he had gambled on cockfights there—and he scouted the terrain. He found that the British had cut down most of the trees outside the town, and then used them to block roads. They had left the tree stumps so that they would be in the way of soldiers moving toward them. Two creeks on either side of town—Yorktown Creek and Wormley Creek—ran to the York River. In between the two was a piece of land known as the gorge; it was a sandy plain, devoid of much vegetation except some thin grass.

After looking things over, Washington decided that Cornwallis could be forced out through a siege.[5] He ordered the big siege guns—cannons and mortars—brought up and put into place. As that was occurring, he received an unexpected present from Cornwallis. Early on the morning of September 30, the British abandoned their outer defenses. Allied troops quickly moved into them, putting them that much closer to the British. It was like winning a battle without firing a single shot.

By October 9, many of the big siege guns were in place. Washington himself fired the first shot to start the siege. Supposedly, the cannonball slammed into a house where some British officers were eating, killing or wounding the officer at the

Although mortars were indirect firing weapons, they could be aimed with deadly accuracy. Because mortars fire in a high arc, they could be used from the safety of a trench, whereas a cannon could not.

Cannons were identified by the weight of the ball that they shot. Thus, a 12-pounder shot a 12-pound ball. Among the allied guns were three 24-pounders and three 18-pounders. These guns were heavy and awkward, and transporting them along uneven dirt roads that were usually either filled with ruts or mud was no easy task. A 12-pounder weighed over 3,000 pounds; it took a team of at least 12 horses to move it.

For a siege, the big guns were brought up to the front lines so that they could be as close as possible to the enemy. Once a cannon was at the front, artillery crews used ropes to drag it into the final position. Placing artillery pieces was dangerous work, particularly if, as the siege progressed, the guns were moved closer and closer to the enemy. Sharpshooters would try to pick off the artillery crews as they worked to move their guns.

Cannons were direct firing weapons, meaning that they were aimed using a direct line of sight between the weapon and the target. Mortars were indirect firing weapons—they were not aimed directly at their target. Instead, they fired projectiles in a high arc. Mortars were easily transportable. They were not on wheels, like cannons, but were placed on wooden beds that served as foundations to hold them.

Mortar   Cannon

The firing from the allied siege was so intense that Cornwallis sought refuge in a cave in Yorktown. This was quite a comedown for a general used to the finer things in life.

head of the table.[6] Thereafter the guns kept up a constant bombardment day and night. Initially there were 46 guns shooting approximately 100 rounds a day, meaning that there were 4,600 cannonballs and other types of shells pouring into the small area where the British were huddled.[7] More guns were added, and the firing became heavier.

By October 11, some allied guns were 360 yards (327 meters) from the British—virtually point-blank range. The constant rain of allied shot and shell forced Cornwallis and his officers to live in caves. Yorktown quickly became a place where no living thing could survive out in the open. Noted one soldier, "The slaughter was great."[8]

The night attack by the allies on Redoubts 9 and 10 on October 14 (see chapter one) was indeed successful. The allies extended their trenches even closer to the British. They also moved guns into the redoubts. The British were boxed in, and the allies relentlessly pounded them.

Meanwhile, in New York, days came and went with no rescue effort. Graves wrote that he would not fight if he could avoid it.[9]

At Yorktown, Cornwallis was coming to grips with how dangerous the town had become. On October 15, he wrote to Clinton: "the safety of the place [Yorktown] is . . . so precarious that I cannot recommend that the fleet and army should run great risk in endeavoring to save us."[10] Then Cornwallis reverted to his fighting ways. On October 16, he had 350 British soldiers attack the allied forces closest to them and spike some of the guns. (They drove an object, usually an iron spike, into the firing holes, rendering them useless.) However, the British were driven back, and the guns were quickly repaired and returned to action. That night Cornwallis tried to escape with his troops across the river to nearby Gloucester—one of his officers called the attempt "a last resort"[11]—but a sudden storm spoiled the attempt.

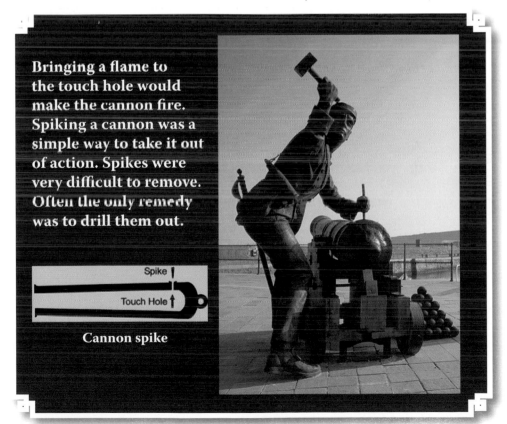

Bringing a flame to the touch hole would make the cannon fire. Spiking a cannon was a simple way to take it out of action. Spikes were very difficult to remove. Often the only remedy was to drill them out.

Spike

Touch Hole

Cannon spike

In *Surrender of Lord Cornwallis*, French officers (left) and American officers, including Washington, (right) watch a British officer surrender to General Benjamin Lincoln.

The next morning, on October 17, 1781, after a brief inspection of the allied positions, Cornwallis asked Washington for surrender terms. On October 19, the British Army formally surrendered to the allies. Claiming illness, Cornwallis sent his deputy, Brigadier General Charles O'Hara, to surrender for him. (The same day, a British rescue force left Sandy Hook, New Jersey, bound for Virginia.)

As the British band played the melancholy tune "The World Turned Upside Down," the British soldiers—about 3,500—formally relinquished their weapons, many of them throwing them down hard on the ground, trying to break them. Some British soldiers were reportedly drunk, some cried, and others were just angry.

By midafternoon, the surrender ceremony was over. The siege of Yorktown had resulted in a great victory for the allies. If ever there was a battle where strategy ruled supreme, Yorktown was it. Barring the siege, who knows how a pitched battle would have gone? In selecting this strategy, Washington had secured victory, and with it he guaranteed the birth of the United States.

Aftermath

Many people think that the surrender at Yorktown ended the American Revolution, but it did not. Fighting continued for nearly two years.

It took until November 25 for the news of Cornwallis's surrender to reach England. When Prime Minister Lord North, an ardent supporter of the war, heard the news, he cried "Oh, God, it is all over!"[12] King George III vowed to continue the war. However, with public support for the war vanishing, the House of Commons voted against continuing the war any further, and authorized the king to make peace with the former colonies in America. With his policies completely rejected, North resigned on March 20, 1782, and a new government took over. The peace treaty, known as the Treaty of Paris, was signed in September 1783.

Benjamin West's painting of the signing of the Treaty of Paris includes Americans (left to right) John Jay, John Adams, Benjamin Franklin, Henry Laurens, and William Temple Franklin. West left room for the British delegation, but they refused to sit for the picture.

After the treaty was signed, Washington disbanded the army. In December, he resigned as commander in chief. He was then called to serve the new nation yet again, first as president of the Constitutional Congress in 1787 and then as the country's first president.

Clinton and Cornwallis took turns blaming each other for the defeat at Yorktown. Cornwallis went on to other military victories; Clinton did not.

All dates 1781

May	British lieutenant general Lord Charles Cornwallis with about 7,500 soldiers enters Virginia after a hard campaign in the American south. A small army under the command of the Marquis de Lafayette opposes him.
August 2	Cornwallis occupies Yorktown.
August 14	George Washington, with his army near New York City, learns that a large French fleet will arrive shortly in Chesapeake Bay. He immediately abandons his plan to attack British-occupied New York to go after Cornwallis in Virginia.
August 19	A French army under the command of Count Rochambeau moves south from Newport, Rhode Island, and joins Washington, bringing the total number of allied forces to about 16,000.
Late August	Washington uses several tricks to deceive Sir Henry Clinton, overall British commander and head of the forces in New York City, into thinking that he is planning to attack the city.
August 30	Washington receives word that the French fleet has arrived in Chesapeake Bay. He abandons deceptive tactics and, along with Rochambeau's men, heads for Virginia. Clinton does not give chase.
September 1	A British fleet of about 19 ships under the command of Admiral Thomas Graves sails from New York to Chesapeake Bay.
September 2–4	The allied armies pass through Philadelphia.
September 5	In the most critical sea battle of the war, the French fleet defeats the British fleet outside Chesapeake Bay. This prevents the British from coming to Cornwallis' rescue in Yorktown.
September 28	The allied troops surround Cornwallis in Yorktown and begin preparations for a siege.
October 9	The allied forces begin the siege. Washington fires the first gun. Artillery pounds the British day and night.
October 14	The allies attack British Redoubts 9 and 10 in a successful night engagement, forcing the British to retreat into a small area in the town of Yorktown.
October 16	Cornwallis tries twice to escape the allies' ever-tightening trap. Both attempts fail.
October 17	Cornwallis asks for surrender terms.
October 19	The British Army formally surrenders. Although the war will go on for two more years, the fighting is effectively over.

1732	James Oglethorpe is granted a charter for Georgia, the last of the thirteen colonies.
1739	The Methodist Church is founded.
1743	The American Philosophical Society is formed in Philadelphia.
1752	Benjamin Franklin invents the lightning rod.
1754	The French and Indian War begins.
1755	Samuel Johnson publishes his famous dictionary of the English language.
1756	The French and Indian War spreads to Europe, where it becomes known as the Seven Years' War.
1760	George III becomes king of England.
1761	The first life insurance policy in America is issued.
1763	The Treaty of Paris is signed, officially ending the Seven Years' War.
1765	British Parliament passes the Stamp Act.
1767	English scientist Joseph Priestley invents carbonated water.
1770	British soldiers fire into a crowd on March 5 in Boston in what will become known as the Boston Massacre.
1775	The battles of Lexington and Concord begin the Revolutionary War.
1781	The planet Uranus is discovered.
1783	The Revolutionary War is officially over.
1789	The French Revolution begins. The guillotine is invented.
1794	Eli Whitney patents the cotton gin.
1801	Great Britain and Ireland merge to form the United Kingdom. Eli Whitney demonstrates muskets with interchangeable parts. His machinery revolutionizes the small-arms industry.
1804	The Lewis and Clark Expedition begins.
1812	The War of 1812 between the United States and Great Britain begins.
1814	George Stephenson designs the first steam locomotive.
1815	Napoleon is defeated at Waterloo.
1819	The United States acquires Florida from Spain.

Chapter 1. Bayonet Night Attack!

1. Martin Davidson and Adam Levy, *Decisive Weapons* (London: BBC Books, 1996), p. 57.
2. Burke Davis, *The Campaign That Won America* (New York: The Dial Press, 1970), p. 202.
3. Thomas J. Fleming, *Beat the Last Drum* (New York: St. Martin's Press, 1963), p. 280.
4. Robert Leckie, *George Washington's War* (New York: HarperCollins Publishers, 1992), p. 657.

Chapter 2. Muskets and Long Rifles

1. Thomas J. Fleming, *Beat the Last Drum* (New York: St. Martin's Press, 1963), p. 6.
2. Richard M. Ketchum, *Victory at Yorktown* (New York: Henry Holt and Company, 2004), p. 88.
3. Ibid., p. 95.
4. Edwin Tunis, *Weapons* (Baltimore: The Johns Hopkins University Press, 1999), p. 101.
5. Fleming, p. 39.
6. Ibid.
7. Burke Davis, *The Campaign That Won America* (New York: The Dial Press, 1970), p. 105.

Chapter 3. Two Strategies

1. Burke Davis, *The Campaign That Won America* (New York: The Dial Press, 1970), p. 5.
2. Robert Leckie, *George Washington's War* (New York: HarperCollins Publishers, 1992), p. 638.
3. Ibid.
4. Davis, p. 17.
5. Ibid., p. 9.
6. John Mollo, *Uniforms of the American Revolution* (New York: Macmillan Publishing Co., Inc, 1975), p. 57.
7. Ibid.
8. Ibid.

Chapter 4. The March South

1. Robert Leckie, *George Washington's War* (New York: HarperCollins Publishers, 1992), p. 640.
2. Burke Davis, *The Campaign That Won America* (New York: The Dial Press, 1970), p. 19.
3. Thomas J. Fleming, *Beat the Last Drum* (New York: St. Martin's Press, 1963), p. 93.
4. Ibid., p. 95.
5. Davis, p. 49.
6. Fleming, p. 163.
7. Ibid., p. 118.
8. Davis, p. 166.

Chapter 5. Siege at Yorktown

1. Burke Davis, *The Campaign That Won America* (New York: The Dial Press, 1970), p. 51.
2. Henry B. Carrington, *Battles of the American Revolution 1775–1781* (New York: Promontory Press; 1904, 2010), p. 631.
3. Ibid.
4. Thomas J. Fleming, *Beat the Last Drum* (New York: St. Martin's Press, 1963), p. 222.
5. Davis, p. 192.
6. Richard M. Ketchum, *Victory at Yorktown* (New York: Henry Holt and Company, 2004), p. 227.
7. Fleming, p. 244.
8. Davis, p. 218.
9. Ibid., p. 250.
10. Ketchum, p. 236.
11. Ibid., p. 237.
12. Robert Leckie, *George Washington's War* (New York: HarperCollins Publishers, 1992), p. 659.

Works Consulted

Carrington, Henry B. *Battles of the American Revolution 1775–1781*. New York: Promontory Press, 1904, 2010.

Davidson, Martin, and Adam Levy. *Decisive Weapons*. London: BBC Books, 1996.

Davis, Burke. *The Campaign That Won America*. New York: The Dial Press, 1970.

Fleming, Thomas J. *Beat the Last Drum*. New York: St. Martin's Press, 1963.

George Washington: A Biography in His Own Words. Ralph K. Andrist, Editor. New York: Newsweek, Inc., 1972.

Hogg, Ian V., and John Batchelor. *Armies of the American Revolution*. Englewood Cliffs, New Jersey: Prentice-Hall Inc., 1975.

Jefferson, Thomas. *Notes on the State of Virginia*. New York: W.W. Norton & Company, Inc., 1972.

Ketchum, Richard M. *Victory at Yorktown*. New York: Henry Holt and Company, 2004.

Leckie, Robert. *George Washington's War*. New York: HarperCollins Publishers, 1992.

Mollo, John. *Uniforms of the American Revolution*. New York: Macmillan Publishing Co., Inc, 1975.

Russell, Carl P. *Guns on the Early Frontiers*. New York: Bonanza Books, 1957.

Tunis, Edwin. *Weapons*. Baltimore: The Johns Hopkins University Press, 1999.

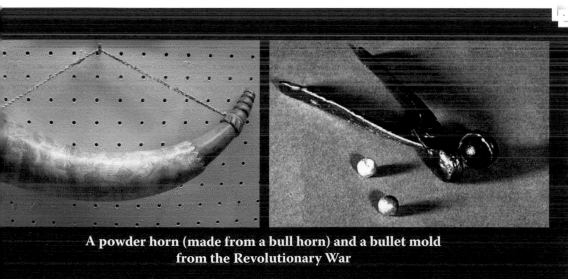

A powder horn (made from a bull horn) and a bullet mold
from the Revolutionary War

Books

Bayam, Michèle. *Arms and Armor*. New York: DK Books, 2004.

Draper, Allison Stark. *The End of the American Revolutionary War: The Colonists Defeat the British at Yorktown*. New York: PowerKids Press, 2000.

Ferrie, Richard. *The World Turned Upside Down: George Washington and the Battle of Yorktown*. New York: Holiday House, 1999.

Fradin, Dennis B. *The Battle of Yorktown*. New York: Marshall Cavendish Benchmark, 2009.

Ready, Dee. *The Battle of Yorktown*. Mankato, Minn., 2002.

Vierow, Wendy. *The Battle of Yorktown*. New York: PowerKids Press, 2003.

On the Internet

British Battles: Battle of Yorktown 1781
http://www.britishbattles.com/battle-yorktown.htm

The History Place: American Revolution
http://www.historyplace.com/unitedstates/revolution

National Park Service Museum Collections, "American Revolutionary War: Guilford Courthouse"—Weapons of War
http://www.nps.gov/history/museum/exhibits/revwar/guco/gucoweapons.html

The Patriot Resource: Battle of Yorktown
http://www.patriotresource.com/amerrev/battles/yorktown.html

The White House: George Washington
http://www.whitehouse.gov/about/presidents/georgewashington

abatis (AA-buh-tis *or* AA-buh-tee)—An obstacle made by felled trees with sharpened branches that face the enemy (the plural is *abatises*—AA-buh-tis-es).

allegiance (uh-LEE-junts)—Loyalty to a person, group, cause, or government.

artillery (ar-TIL-uh-ree)—Weapons that fire projectiles, such as bullets or arrows; also, mounted firearms for larger projectiles.

bayonet (bay-uh-NET)—A steel blade that attaches to the end of a musket or rifle for use in hand-to-hand combat.

comte (KOMPT)—French for "count," a nobleman.

confidant (KON-fih-dahnt)—A person with whom secrets are shared.

flintlock—A lock for a gun or pistol that holds a piece of flint; the hammer strikes the flint and causes a spark, which ignites the charge. Also, a gun or pistol fitted with such a lock.

maritime (MAR-ih-tym)—Relating to the sea or to navigation of the sea.

maul (MALL)—To beat, mangle, or handle roughly.

mortar (MOR-tur)—A short-barreled heavy gun used for launching shells at high angles.

musket (MUS-kit)—A heavy, large gun used by infantry soldiers.

muzzleloader (MUH-zul-loh-der)—A musket, pistol, or long gun in which bullets are loaded from the front of the barrel.

redoubt (rih-DOWT)—A small usually temporary structure used for defense in battle.

rifling (RYF-ling)—The grooves on the inside of a gun barrel that make a bullet spin on its way out.

siege (SEEJ)—A military blockade set up to force a city or fort to surrender.

smoothbore (SMOOTH-bor)—A firearm with an unrifled barrel.

stock—The rear part of a gun.

vacillate (VAS-ih-layt)—To waver when trying to make a decision.

Index